LE CORDON BLEU

HOME COLLECTION

·CHRISTMAS·

MURDOCH BOOKS®

Sydney • London • Vancouver • New York

contents

recipe ratings ✲ easy ✲✲ a little more care needed ✲✲✲ more care needed

Colcannon and smoked chicken canapés

*These delicious appetizers of smoky chicken and cranberry chutney have an Irish twist,
with a filling of buttery potato and cabbage.*

Preparation time 35 minutes + 30 minutes refrigeration
Total cooking time 45 minutes
Makes 24

PASTRY
200 g (6¹/2 oz) plain flour
¹/4 teaspoon salt
40 g (1¹/4 oz) unsalted butter, chilled and cut
    into cubes
2 egg yolks
3 tablespoons water

COLCANNON
120 g (4 oz) floury potatoes
55 g (1³/4 oz) cabbage
1 tablespoon oil
¹/2 small onion, finely chopped
60 g (2 oz) smoked chicken, finely chopped

CRANBERRY CHUTNEY
55 g (1³/4 oz) cranberries, fresh or frozen
2 teaspoons soft brown sugar
2 teaspoons white wine vinegar

1 Brush two 12-hole shallow patty pans or tart trays or 24 individual tartlet tins, 3 cm (1¹/4 inches) across and 1.5 cm (⁵/8 inch) deep, with some melted butter.

2 To make the pastry, sieve together the flour and salt into a large bowl. Using your fingertips, rub the butter into the flour until the mixture resembles fine breadcrumbs. Make a well in the centre and add the egg yolks and water. Work the mixture together with a palette knife until it forms a rough ball. Turn out onto a lightly floured work surface, form into a ball and cover with plastic wrap. Chill in the refrigerator for 20 minutes.

3 Preheat the oven to warm 170°C (325°F/Gas 3). Roll out the dough between two sheets of greaseproof paper to a thickness of 2 mm (¹/8 inch). Using a round cutter slightly larger than the holes in the patty pans, cut out 24 rounds. Place the rounds in each pan, pressing down on the bottom so that the dough extends slightly above the edge of the holes. Place in the refrigerator to chill for 10 minutes. Lightly prick the base of the pastry and bake for 12–15 minutes, or until lightly browned, then cool completely before use.

4 To make the colcannon, place the potatoes in a pan of salted, cold water, cover and bring to the boil. Reduce the heat and simmer for about 15–20 minutes, or until the potatoes are tender to the point of a sharp knife. Drain, return to the pan and shake over low heat for 1–2 minutes to remove excess moisture. Mash or push through a fine sieve into a bowl and season with salt and black pepper.

5 Place the cabbage in a pan of salted, cold water and bring to the boil. Blanch for 1 minute, then remove and finely chop. Heat the oil in a frying pan, add the onion and cook for 1 minute over high heat, stirring occasionally. Add the potato and cabbage and stir to combine with the onion. Continue cooking over medium heat for 10 minutes, or until the mixture has a mottled brown appearance, then add the chicken, season with salt and black pepper and keep warm.

6 To make the cranberry chutney, place the cranberries, sugar, vinegar and 1 tablespoon water into a small pan. Bring slowly to the boil, stirring to dissolve the sugar, then raise the heat to medium and simmer for about 5–10 minutes, or until the mixture is almost dry and is thick and reduced. Remove from the heat and set aside.

7 Fill the cooled tartlets with a teaspoon of the colcannon and top with a small amount of the chutney. Arrange on a platter and serve warm or cold.

Blue cheese and tomato canapés

Serve warm while the cheese is still melting and these canapés will disappear in an instant.

Preparation time **15 minutes**
Total cooking time **20 minutes**
Makes 60

☗

15 thin slices day-old white or brown bread
2¹/₂ tablespoons tomato paste
200 g (6¹/₂ oz) firm blue cheese, such as Stilton, crumbled
1¹/₂ tablespoons chopped fresh basil or oregano

1 Preheat the oven to moderately hot 190°C (375°F/ Gas 5). Using a 4 cm (1¹/2 inch) plain pastry cutter, cut out four circles from each slice of bread, discarding the trimmings. Place the rounds on two baking trays and bake for about 15 minutes, turning them halfway through cooking.
2 Spread the rounds with the tomato paste and put them back on the baking trays. Cover each one with blue cheese and sprinkle with half the basil or oregano. Return to the oven for 2 minutes, or until the cheese just starts to melt, but is not so liquid that it runs off the canapés. Season with black pepper, sprinkle with the remaining herbs and serve immediately.

Chef's tips For a variation, other blue cheeses such as Roquefort can be used, but will give a much stronger salty taste.

To prepare ahead of time, cool the bread circles after baking. Just before serving, spread with the tomato paste and top with the cheese and herbs. Either cook in the oven or under a preheated grill at the highest setting to melt the cheese and heat them through.

Beef and horseradish canapés

A classic combination of roast beef and horseradish sauce in bite-size portions.

Preparation time **15 minutes**
Total cooking time **5 minutes**
Makes 32

☗

8 thin slices day-old white or brown bread
150 g (5 oz) rare roasted beef, finely chopped
30 g (1 oz) fresh horseradish, finely grated
   or 2 teaspoons horseradish cream
60 ml (2 fl oz) cream, lightly whipped or sour cream
fresh chervil sprigs, to garnish

1 Preheat the grill. Using a 4 cm (1¹/2 inch) plain pastry cutter, cut out four circles from each slice of bread and discard the trimmings. Toast the circles on each side under the grill and remove to a cooling rack.
2 Place the chopped beef in a bowl and mix in the horseradish and cream. Season with salt and black pepper, bearing in mind the heat of the horseradish.
3 Using a teaspoon, mound the beef mixture neatly onto the cooled rounds of bread and garnish with a small sprig of chervil.

Chef's tip For a variation, use the same ingredients as above, but do not chop the beef. Mix the horseradish, lightly whipped cream and salt and black pepper in a bowl. Pipe or spoon onto the toast, then place thinly sliced rounds of beef on top, dust half the canapés with paprika and place a fan or thin slice of gherkin on the other half.

Blue cheese and tomato canapés (left) and Beef and horseradish canapés

Honey-glazed spiced ham

A whole ham is perfect for feeding a large Christmas gathering. This version is served hot with a mustard cream sauce, but any leftovers make a delicious Boxing Day lunch with a green salad and pickles.

Preparation time **30 minutes + overnight soaking**
Total cooking time **6 hours**
Serves 20

7 kg (14 lb) uncooked leg of ham, smoked or
   unsmoked
2 onions
2 celery sticks
3 carrots
3–4 bay leaves
3 sprigs fresh thyme
1 clove
4 allspice

HONEY GLAZE
125 g (4 oz) soft brown or demerara sugar
105 g (3 1/2 oz) honey
1 1/2 teaspoons ground mixed spice
1 tablespoon English mustard
cloves, for decoration

MUSTARD CREAM SAUCE
500 ml (16 fl oz) thick (double) cream
75 g (2 1/2 oz) English mustard
25 g (3/4 oz) whole mustard seeds, soaked in water

1 Soak the ham overnight in cold water, changing the water once or twice.

2 Preheat the oven to warm 160°C (315°F/Gas 2–3). Tip off the soaking liquid from the ham and rinse it under cold water. Pat dry, place in a large roasting pan and distribute the vegetables, herbs and spices around it. Pour 500 ml (16 fl oz) cold water into the pan and cover the pan with foil. Bake for 20 minutes per 500 g (1 lb), then cook for an extra 20 minutes.

3 Remove the ham from the oven and lift it out of the liquid. Reserve the cooking liquid and discard the vegetables. To prepare the ham, follow the method in the Chef's techniques on page 61. Raise the oven temperature to moderate 180°C (350°F/Gas 4).

4 To make the honey glaze, mix all the ingredients except the cloves together in a bowl and spread over the ham with a palette knife. Push a clove into the centre of each diamond. Place, fat-side-up, on a rack over a roasting pan into which 1 cm (1/2 inch) water has been poured (this will make the pan easier to clean later on). Bake the ham for 20 minutes, or until the surface is lightly caramelized. Rest for 30 minutes before carving.

5 To make the mustard cream sauce, boil the ham's cooking liquid in a pan over high heat for 30 minutes, or until reduced to a light syrup. Add the cream and return to the boil, then remove from the heat and stir in the mustard and drained mustard seeds. Do not reboil or the mustard will lose its fresh flavour. Taste and season only if necessary.

6 To carve the ham, follow the method in the Chef's techniques on page 61. Serve the ham with the hot mustard cream sauce, some new potatoes and a selection of vegetables.

Chef's tips If you want to serve the ham cold, allow to cool after removing from the oven. Rather than serving with the hot mustard cream sauce, mix 250 g (8 oz) mayonnaise with 30 g (1 oz) wholegrain mustard to accompany the ham. Serve with hot new potatoes, mixed salad leaves and pickles or chutneys.

If a whole ham is too big, use a half ham or piece of boned gammon. Cook in the same way, calculating the cooking time at 30 minutes per 500 g (1 lb).

Roast turkey with bread sauce and gravy

The classic Christmas dinner: a golden turkey with bread sauce and gravy. The turkey needs about 2 hours cooking time and can then sit for up to 45 minutes while the juices seep back into the meat to keep it moist.

Preparation time **35 minutes**
Total cooking time **2 hours 50 minutes**
   + 30 minutes standing
Serves 8

**1 x 6 kg (12 lb) turkey, plus the neck from the
   giblets if available**
105 ml (3¹/2 fl oz) vegetable oil
watercress, to garnish

GRAVY
1 small onion, roughly chopped
1 small carrot, roughly chopped
2 celery sticks, roughly chopped
30 g (1 oz) plain flour
500 ml (16 fl oz) chicken stock

BREAD SAUCE
600 ml (20 fl oz) milk
¹/2 onion, studded with 3–4 cloves
1 bouquet garni (see Chef's tip)
2 cloves garlic, peeled and lightly bruised
105 g (3¹/2 oz) fresh white breadcrumbs
grated fresh nutmeg
**2¹/2 tablespoons cream or 45 g (1¹/2 oz) unsalted
   butter, optional**

1 Clean the turkey inside and out, removing any feathers. With a sharp knife, cut off and reserve the end wing joints. Lift up the flap of skin at the neck and, using a small sharp knife, scrape the meat away from the wishbone and remove the wishbone. Tie the legs together with string. Preheat the oven to moderate 180°C (350°F/Gas 4).
2 Place a large roasting pan over medium heat and heat the oil. Add the end wing joints and neck and cook until lightly browned, then arrange the turkey on top and bake for 1¹/2–2 hours, basting with the juices and oil every 20 minutes. If the turkey begins to overbrown, cover with foil. The turkey is cooked if the juices run clear when you pierce a leg and thigh with a skewer. If pink, continue roasting until the juices are clear. Transfer the turkey to a large plate and leave in a warm place.
3 To make the gravy, tip off the excess fat from the pan, retaining about a tablespoon with all the juices. Add the onion, carrot and celery and cook over moderate heat, stirring occasionally, for 3–5 minutes, or until tender. Sprinkle on the flour, then stir in to mix evenly and cook for 1 minute. Add the stock gradually and stir over low heat to produce a smooth texture. Bring to the boil, then reduce the heat and simmer for 10 minutes. Strain, skim off the excess fat and season with some salt and black pepper.
4 To make the bread sauce, pour the milk into a small pan, add the onion, bouquet garni and garlic and bring slowly just to the boil. Remove from the heat and leave to stand for 20–30 minutes. Strain and discard the flavourings, then return the milk to the pan and bring to the boil. Whisk in the breadcrumbs to produce a thick sauce and season with the nutmeg and some salt and black pepper. Stir in the cream or butter. Serve immediately, as the sauce will thicken on standing.
5 To carve the turkey, follow the method in the Chef's techniques on page 61. Serve with the bread sauce, gravy, stuffing and other traditional accompaniments (see pages 12–15).

Chef's tip To make a bouquet garni, wrap the green part of a leek loosely around a bay leaf, a sprig of thyme, some celery leaves and a few stalks of parsley, then tie with string, leaving a long tail for easy removal.

Chestnut and pork stuffing balls

A traditional stuffing mixture of chestnuts and pork sausage meat.

*Preparation time **20 minutes***
*Total cooking time **35 minutes***
Serves 8–10

60 g (2 oz) unsalted butter
1 onion
2 large cloves garlic, chopped
210 g (6³/4 oz) cooked, peeled chestnuts (fresh, canned or frozen), chopped
2 tablespoons chopped fresh parsley
60 g (2 oz) fresh white breadcrumbs
600 g (1¹/4 lb) pork sausage meat
2 teaspoons finely grated lemon rind
1 tablespoon lemon juice
2 eggs, beaten
2 tablespoons vegetable oil or dripping

1 Heat the butter in a pan and add the onion and garlic. Cook, covered, over low heat for 5 minutes, or until translucent. Remove from the heat and cool. Preheat the oven to moderate 180°C (350°F/Gas 4).
2 Place the onion and garlic in a bowl and add the chestnuts, parsley, breadcrumbs, sausage meat, lemon rind and juice. Mix well and season with salt and black pepper. Add the egg and mix in thoroughly.
3 Turn the mixture onto a lightly floured surface. Using floured hands, roll into a sausage shape about 4 cm (1¹/2 inches) in diameter. Cut into 18 pieces and roll each piece into a ball. Grease a baking dish with the oil or dripping and add the balls in a single layer. Bake for 30 minutes, or until golden, then drain on crumpled paper towels.

Sage and onion stuffing with bacon chipolatas

A simple sage and onion stuffing and a well-loved accompaniment to turkey: bacon-wrapped sausages.

*Preparation time **30 minutes***
*Total cooking time **1 hour 5 minutes***
Serves 8

80 g (2³/4 oz) unsalted butter
1 small onion, finely chopped
2 cloves garlic, finely chopped or crushed
2 tablespoons finely chopped fresh sage leaves
150 g (5 oz) fresh white breadcrumbs
1 egg, beaten
30 g (1 oz) unsalted butter, at room temperature

BACON CHIPOLATAS
16 thin rashers of speck or streaky bacon
16 chipolatas or small sausages

1 Preheat the oven to moderate 180°C (350°F/Gas 4). Heat the butter in a pan and add the onion and garlic. Cook, covered, over low heat for 5 minutes, or until translucent. Add the sage and cook gently for 1 minute. Remove from the heat and stir in the breadcrumbs, salt and black pepper, then mix in the egg.
2 Using your fingers, spread a 25 x 50 cm (10 x 20 inch) foil strip with the butter. Place the stuffing down the centre of the foil's length, leaving 8 cm (3 inches) of foil without stuffing at each end. Fold the foil over to enclose the stuffing and form a long roll, then twist the ends of the foil in opposite directions to tighten to a flat sausage shape. Place on a baking tray and bake for 30–40 minutes. Slice into thick slices to serve.
3 To make the bacon chipolatas, stretch out the bacon and wrap a piece around each sausage. Secure with a cocktail stick. Place in a baking dish and bake for 20 minutes, turning once. Remove the cocktail sticks before serving.

Chestnut and pork stuffing balls (left) and Sage and onion stuffing with bacon chipolatas

Roast potatoes

Meals involving roasted meats are never quite the same without crisp, golden roast potatoes. Even the simplest ingredients—olive oil, rosemary or salt—will further enhance their wonderful flavour.

*Preparation time **15 minutes***
*Total cooking time **50 minutes***
Serves 4

1 kg (2 lb) floury potatoes
oil, for cooking

1 Preheat the oven to moderately hot 190°C (375°F/Gas 5). Peel the potatoes and cut them into evenly sized pieces—halve or quarter them depending on their size. Place in a large pan of salted water, bring to the boil, then reduce the heat and simmer for about 5 minutes. Drain, then while the potatoes are still hot, hold each one in a cloth and lightly scratch the surface with a fork. Return to the pan and cover to keep hot.
2 Preheat a roasting pan over high heat and add oil to a depth of about 1 cm (^{1}/2 inch). As the oil just starts to smoke, add the potatoes in a single layer. Roll them in the hot oil to seal all sides. Bake for 40 minutes, or until the potatoes are golden, turning and basting frequently with the oil. Drain on crumpled paper towels, sprinkle with salt and serve while still hot.

Chef's tips King Edward, spunta and sebago potatoes are perfect for roasting.

Boiling potatoes prior to roasting removes excess sticky starch from the surface, leaving them dry and crisp; scratching the surface contributes texture to that crispness. Rolling hot potatoes in hot oil will then seal them nicely, leaving the centres floury and oil free.

If the potatoes are to accompany a roasted meat, instead of cooking them in a separate pan, place them in the hot fat around the meat as it cooks. This will give added flavour.

Roasted parsnips with honey and ginger

A very popular vegetable in Ancient Greece and during the Middle Ages and the Renaissance, the parsnip has a lovely sweet flavour.

*Preparation time **10 minutes***
*Total cooking time **20 minutes***
Serves 6

6 parsnips, about 750 g (1^1/2 lb)
60 ml (2 fl oz) oil
15 g (^{1}/2 oz) unsalted butter
1 tablespoon clear honey
1 tablespoon finely grated or chopped fresh ginger

1 Preheat the oven to hot 220°C (425°F/Gas 7). Cut the peeled parsnips in half lengthways, or quarters if they are large, to make pieces about 8 cm (3 inches) long and 2.5 cm (1 inch) thick. Remove any woody cores. Put in a large pan and cover with water. Add a pinch of salt and bring to the boil over high heat. Boil for 1 minute before draining. Return to the saucepan and dry well by shaking the pan over low heat for about 1 minute.
2 Heat the oil in a roasting pan on the stove. Add the parsnips and cook quickly over high heat, turning to colour evenly. Add the butter to the pan, transfer to the oven for 10 minutes. Spoon or tip out the excess oil.
3 Add the honey and ginger, turning the parsnips to coat evenly, and roast for another 5 minutes.
4 Lift the parsnips out of the pan and serve hot.

Roast potatoes (left) with Roasted parsnips with honey and ginger

Loin of pork with prunes and Armagnac

This recipe for roast pork has a strong Christmas flavour to it, with a stuffing of sweet prunes and French brandy. Loin of pork is a cut that is easy to carve into neat slices.

*Preparation time **30 minutes + 1 hour soaking***
*Total cooking time **1 hour 50 minutes***
Serves 4–6

60 g (2 oz) pitted prunes
1¹/2 tablespoons Armagnac
1.5 kg (3 lb) boned loin of pork, with a long
   rib flap if possible
2 teaspoons oil
15 g (¹/2 oz) unsalted butter

HERB SAUCE
35 g (1¹/4 oz) unsalted butter
2 large French shallots, chopped
500 ml (16 fl oz) chicken stock
225 ml (7¹/4 fl oz) cream
1¹/2 tablespoons finely chopped fresh sage
1¹/2 tablespoons finely chopped fresh parsley

1 Put the prunes in a bowl and pour in the Armagnac. Cover and soak for at least 1 hour.
2 Preheat the oven to moderately hot 200°C (400°F/ Gas 6). Remove the skin and excess sinew from the pork, leaving a thin layer of fat. Open the loin out and on the side of the round muscle of meat where it joins the flat flap that once held the ribs, cut a long slit down the length of the muscle to halfway through the meat.

Remove the prunes from the Armagnac, reserving the Armagnac, and gently push them into the slit, then close and roll the flat flap around the loin. Tie pieces of string 2.5 cm (1 inch) apart along the loin to hold it together. Heat the oil in a frying pan, add the butter and heat until frothy. Add the pork and fry over medium-high heat for 5–8 minutes, or until sealed and browned all over. Transfer to an ovenproof dish or roasting pan and bake for 1–1¹/4 hours, or until the juices run clear when pierced with a skewer.

3 To make the herb sauce, melt the butter in a pan, add the shallots and cook, covered, over low heat for about 5 minutes, or until soft and translucent. Add the reserved Armagnac and cook, uncovered, until reduced to about 1 tablespoon. Pour in the stock and simmer for 15–20 minutes, or until reduced to ¹/4 cup (60 ml/2 fl oz), then stir in the cream and simmer until the sauce lightly coats the back of a spoon. Remove from the heat, cover the surface with plastic wrap and keep warm.

4 Remove the pork from the oven and transfer to a plate to rest for 5 minutes, then place on a chopping board. Gently reheat the sauce, but do not allow it to bubble for more than 1 minute. Add the sage and parsley and season with salt and black pepper just before serving. Remove the string from the meat and, using a thin, sharp knife, cut the pork into slices. Arrange the slices on plates and pour the sauce around. Serve with a green salad or vegetables and potatoes.

Roast quail

This small game bird makes a lovely choice for a special Christmas dinner, with a whole quail for each guest. Here they are stuffed with a rice and bacon filling and served with a wine sauce.

*Preparation time **1 hour***
*Total cooking time **1 hour***
Serves 4

RICE AND BACON STUFFING
30 g (1 oz) unsalted butter
1 onion, finely chopped
85 g (2³/4 oz) basmati rice
55 g (1³/4 oz) speck or streaky bacon, diced
1 tablespoon finely chopped fresh flat-leaf parsley
2 teaspoons sultanas or raisins

4 quails
1 tablespoon peanut or groundnut oil
45 g (1¹/2 oz) unsalted butter

WINE SAUCE
30 g (1 oz) unsalted butter
2 French shallots, finely chopped
100 ml (3¹/4 fl oz) sweet white wine, such as Sauternes
250 ml (8 fl oz) chicken or veal stock

1 To make the rice and bacon stuffing, melt the butter in a pan, add the onion and cook, covered, over low heat for 5 minutes, or until soft and translucent. Add the rice and 140 ml (4¹/2 fl oz) water. Bring to the boil, then reduce the heat and cook, covered, for 15–20 minutes, or until the rice has absorbed all the water. Remove from the heat and set aside. Heat a small heavy-based pan, add the speck or bacon and dry-fry until golden brown. Add to the rice with any fat that has run out. Stir in the parsley and sultanas, season with salt and black pepper, then set aside to cool.

2 Bone the quails following the method in the Chef's techniques on page 62. Preheat the oven to moderately hot 200°C (400°F/Gas 6). Lay the boned quails out flat, skin-side-down, season lightly with salt and black pepper, then spoon the stuffing into the centre of each bird. Draw the neck skin down over the stuffing and the sides in to cover. Hold the two cut edges of skin and zig-zag a cocktail stick through their length to hold them together. Turn the quail over and, using the side of your little finger, gently plump the body cavity and make a division between it and the legs to give a good shape. Tuck the wing tips under at the neck end and pull the ends of the legs together by skewering through the thighs with a cocktail stick.

3 Heat the oil in a baking tray over medium heat, add the butter and, when melted and foamy, put in the quails, breast-side-down, and the reserved carcass bones. Turn to brown the quails and bones evenly on all sides, then bake for 15 minutes, basting every 5 minutes with the pan juices. Lift the quails and bones onto a plate and leave for 5 minutes.

4 To make the wine sauce, melt the butter in a pan, add the shallots and roasted quail bones and cook for about 1 minute, then add the wine and cook for 5 minutes, or until the liquid has reduced by about three quarters. Pour in the stock and continue to reduce by half. Skim off any excess fat from the pan, then strain the sauce and season with salt and black pepper. Cover the surface with a piece of plastic wrap to stop the sauce from forming a skin and keep warm.

5 To serve, remove and discard the cocktail sticks, cut off the wing tip joints and place the birds on a platter or plates. Spoon the sauce around and serve with vegetables.

Chef's tip Quails vary in size, so if you have some stuffing left over, place it in a lightly buttered small ovenproof dish, cover with buttered foil and cook in the oven with the quails.

Poached salmon with cucumber scales

A dish that can be prepared well before your guests arrive, a whole poached salmon is a striking centrepiece and is delicious served with potatoes and a green salad.

*Preparation time **1 hour 30 minutes***
*Total cooking time **1 hour***
Serves 12

☗ ☗

1 large onion, diced

1 large carrot, diced

2 celery sticks, diced

sprig of fresh thyme

4–5 fresh parsley stalks

1 bay leaf

6 peppercorns

1 teaspoon rock salt or sea salt

1–2 tablespoons white wine vinegar

500 ml (16 fl oz) white wine

1.5–1.75 kg (3–3 1/2 lb) whole fresh salmon, cleaned and scaled (ask your fishmonger to gut the fish and remove the scales)

2 telegraph cucumbers, to garnish

watercress, to garnish

mayonnaise, to serve

1 To make the poaching liquid, place 2 litres water, the vegetables, herbs, peppercorns, salt, vinegar and wine in a large pan. Bring to the boil, then reduce the heat and simmer, covered, for 30 minutes. Strain and discard the solids. Leave to cool.

2 To prepare the salmon for poaching, follow the method in the Chef's techniques on page 60. If you have a fish kettle, lay the salmon on the rack of the kettle and pour over the poaching liquid. Cover and bring to the boil, then reduce the heat to barely simmering and poach for 5–6 minutes per 500 g (1 lb). Remove the pan from the stove and leave the salmon to cool in the liquid.

3 If you do not have a fish kettle, preheat the oven to moderate 180°C (350°F/Gas 4) and prepare the fish following the method in the Chef's techniques on page 60. Bake for about 30 minutes, or until the fish feels firm and the flesh inside looks cooked. Leave the salmon to cool in the liquid.

4 If the salmon has been cooked in the oven, tip off the poaching liquid and lift the fish out and onto a sheet of greaseproof paper. If the salmon has been cooked in the kettle, lift the fish from the kettle using the rack and carefully slide it onto a piece of greaseproof paper. Roll the fish over so the flatter side is on the top. Prepare the salmon for serving following the method in the Chef's techniques on page 60.

5 Slice the cucumber thinly and cover the salmon with overlapping slices of cucumber to give it a new skin of cucumber 'scales'. If you have left the head on, cover the eye with a black olive. Garnish the dish with the watercress. Serve with some mayonnaise, potatoes and a mixed green salad.

Chef's tip Always ensure that the side of salmon that was underneath during cooking is so when served. The weight of the fish above flattens it, so the top side will be plumper and more attractive.

Breast of duck with winter vegetables

A great alternative to roast turkey for a small, grown-up Christmas lunch, especially if you don't want lots of leftovers. Delicious served with a home-made cranberry sauce.

Preparation time **40 minutes**
Total cooking time **35 minutes**
Serves 4

4 duck breasts, about 185 g (6 oz) each
100 g (3¼ oz) parsnips, cut into matchsticks
120 g (4 oz) small Brussels sprouts
155 g (5 oz) celeriac, cut into large cubes
100 g (3¼ oz) sweet potato, cut into large cubes
80 ml (2¾ fl oz) vegetable oil
155 g (5 oz) unsalted butter
120 g (4 oz) tinned chestnuts, halved
4 French shallots, chopped
220 ml (7 fl oz) balsamic vinegar
220 ml (7 fl oz) chicken stock
sprigs fresh rosemary, to garnish

1 Remove any feathers or stubble from the duck breasts, keeping the skin intact. Using a small, sharp knife, trim away and discard any shiny white skin or sinew from the flesh side, then pat dry on paper towels. Lightly score a crisscross pattern in the skin to allow fat to run out during cooking, then season with salt and black pepper.

2 Bring a small pan of water to the boil and separately cook the parsnip for 1 minute, then the sprouts, celeriac and sweet potato for 2 minutes, or until just tender. Lift each out with a slotted spoon into a colander and run a few drops of cold water through each layer to stop the cooking. Drain well.

3 Heat half the oil in a large frying pan, add half the butter and, when melted and foaming, add the chestnuts and drained vegetables and fry for 7 minutes, or until golden. Season with salt and black pepper, remove from the pan and keep warm.

4 Heat the remaining oil and butter in the frying pan and add the duck breasts, skin-side-down. Cook over medium heat for 7 minutes, then turn over and cook for a further 2–3 minutes, or until the skin is crisp and the duck flesh succulent but still slightly pink in the centre.

5 Remove the duck from the pan and set aside in a warm place. Tip the excess fat from the pan, leaving about 1 teaspoon behind with any duck juices. Add the shallots and cook gently for 3 minutes, or until soft, then pour in the balsamic vinegar and boil for 1–2 minutes, or until reduced by one third. Add the stock and cook for 3–4 minutes, or until reduced again by one third. Season with some salt and black pepper and strain the sauce into a jug and keep warm.

6 To serve, slice the duck breasts diagonally into thin slices and serve with the vegetables and sauce. Garnish with small sprigs of rosemary and accompany with cranberry sauce or a chutney.

Chef's tip The duck breasts may also be served whole, especially if you need to keep them warm while eating a first course.

Date-stuffed breast of chicken with Madeira sauce

Relatively quick to prepare, this dish would make a wonderful Christmas Eve dinner. The date and pistachio stuffing and rich Madeira sauce prevent the chicken breast from drying out.

Preparation time **45 minutes**
Total cooking time **50 minutes**
Serves 4

DATE STUFFING
30 g (1 oz) unsalted butter
60 g (2 oz) French shallots, finely chopped
85 g (2³/4 oz) stoned dates
75 g (2¹/2 oz) shelled pistachios, skinned and roughly chopped

4 chicken breasts with skin on (see Chef's tip)
30 g (1 oz) unsalted butter or 1¹/2 tablespoons oil
fresh chervil or parsley, to garnish

MADEIRA SAUCE
250 g (8 oz) French shallots, thinly sliced
200 ml (6¹/2 fl oz) Madeira wine
500 ml (16 fl oz) chicken stock
90 ml (3 fl oz) cream, optional
2 tablespoons chopped fresh chives

1 To make the date stuffing, heat the butter in a small pan and cook the shallots over low heat for 4 minutes, or until soft but not coloured. Finely chop all but three of the dates. Remove the shallots from the heat and stir in the chopped dates and pistachios, then set aside to cool. Preheat the oven to moderate 180°C (350°F/Gas 4).

2 Remove the thin fillets (tenderloins) from the underside of the chicken breasts and place them between lightly oiled pieces of plastic wrap. Gently flatten them with a cutlet bat or small heavy-based pan. On the underside of the breasts, cut a central horizontal slit to half the depth of the flesh. Slide the knife flat inside the slit and to each side to form a pocket, then fill each pocket with the stuffing. Remove the plastic wrap from the small fillets. Place a fillet lengthways on each breast to cover the filling, bringing the edges of the pocket flesh over to seal, then secure with cocktail sticks by pushing them through across the top of the seal. Season with salt and black pepper.

3 Heat the butter or oil in a large frying pan and place the chicken in the pan, skin-side-down. Cook over high heat for 4 minutes, or until just golden. Lift the chicken into a baking tray or shallow ovenproof dish and bake, skin-side-up, for 10–12 minutes, or until the juices from the thickest part of the flesh run clear when pierced with a skewer.

4 To make the Madeira sauce, use the pan and oil the chicken was fried in to cook the shallots over medium-high heat, turning frequently, for 15 minutes, or until golden brown. Tip off any excess fat and pour in three quarters of the Madeira. Bring to the boil, then reduce the heat and simmer for about 3–5 minutes, or until reduced to 2 tablespoons of light syrupy liquid. Add the stock and simmer until reduced by three quarters, then stir in the remaining Madeira and cream, if using. Reduce once again to a light coating consistency. Season with some salt and black pepper, then strain the sauce through a fine sieve into a jug. Stir in the chives, cover and keep warm.

5 Cut the reserved dates lengthways into quarters. Lift the chicken onto a chopping board, remove the cocktail sticks and cut on the diagonal into slices. Lift and fan out on four plates, pour the sauce around and garnish with the dates and a sprig of chervil or parsley. Serve with green vegetables and new potatoes.

Chef's tip If you can't find chicken breast fillets with skin on, then buy breasts on the bone and, using a small sharp knife, fillet the breast.

Vegetable gateaux

These pretty layered vegetable bakes make a good accompaniment to a festive dinner, or can be prepared in advance and served on Christmas Day, with a rich tomato sauce or pesto, for any vegetarian guests.

*Preparation time **25 minutes + 30 minutes standing***
*Total cooking time **35 minutes***
Serves 4

I small thin eggplant (aubergine), sliced into
*   3 mm (¹/8 inch) circles*
30 g (I oz) rock salt
2–3 zucchini (courgettes), cut into 5 mm
*   (¹/4 inch) diagonal slices*
80 ml (2³/4 fl oz) olive oil
I teaspoon chopped fresh thyme
I fennel bulb
I red onion, finely sliced

1 Layer the eggplant slices in a colander, sprinkling rock salt between the layers as they go in. Top with a plate smaller than the colander to press the slices lightly, stand in a bowl and leave for 30 minutes.

2 Place the zucchini in a bowl, add half the oil and the thyme and toss to coat. With a small sharp knife, remove the woody stalks at the top of the fennel bulb. With a large knife, cut the bulb in half from the top and down through the root. Cut away the root from each half then cut the fennel into 5 mm (¹/4 inch) slices.

3 Preheat the oven to moderately hot 200°C (400°F/ Gas 6). In the colander, rinse the eggplant, then dry well on paper towels. Heat a heavy-based frying pan, lightly brush with some of the remaining oil and cook the eggplant for 10 minutes, or until tender. Remove from the pan and place in a bowl. Add a little more oil if necessary, then cook the onion for 2 minutes, or until tender and remove to a separate bowl. Cook the fennel in batches for about 10 minutes, or until tender and remove to a bowl. Finally, cook the zucchini for about 5 minutes, or until tender.

4 Place four metal rings, 10 x 3.5 cm (4 x 1¹/4 inches), or four 150 ml (5 fl oz) ramekins on a baking tray. If using ramekins, cut a disc of foil or baking paper and place in the base of each.

5 Beginning and ending with eggplant, fill the rings or ramekins neatly with layers of the vegetables, draining off any excess oil and seasoning with salt and black pepper between the layers. Bake for about 6–8 minutes to heat through.

6 If using rings, lift the gateaux onto a plate and carefully remove the hot metal rings. If in ramekins, turn out onto a serving plate. Serve as a side dish or as a main-course dish with a thick tomato sauce or pesto.

Chef's tips These gateaux can be prepared in advance and simply heated through in the oven when required.

They are also excellent served hot as a first course with a beurre blanc, hollandaise sauce or a red capsicum (pepper) coulis. Alternatively, serve cold with a herb mayonnaise and crusty bread.

Pumpkin purée

A purée works beautifully with meat dishes that have a lot of sauce to soak up. You could use parsnip or swede instead of the pumpkin.

*Preparation time **10 minutes***
*Total cooking time **30 minutes***
Serves 4

**1 kg (2 lb) butternut pumpkin, peeled and chopped
    into 5 cm (2 inch) cubes**
**50 g (1³/4 oz) unsalted butter, chilled and
    cut into cubes**
60 ml (2 fl oz) thick (double) cream
pinch of freshly grated nutmeg

1 Bring a large pan of salted water to the boil, add the pumpkin cubes, then reduce the heat and simmer for 15–20 minutes, or until the pumpkin is tender to the point of a sharp knife. Drain well and return to the pan. Shake the pan over low heat for about 1 minute to dry out the pumpkin.

2 Pass the pumpkin through a mouli sieve or food processor to purée finely, then return to a clean pan and, over low heat, beat in the butter followed by the cream. Add the nutmeg and some salt and black pepper and serve with meat, fish or poultry.

Gratin of root vegetables

Root vegetables go well with roast meats and this gratin baked with a golden Gruyère topping is a perfect match for a simple roast.

*Preparation time **30 minutes***
*Total cooking time **45 minutes***
Serves 4

30 g (1 oz) unsalted butter
1 clove garlic, finely chopped
250 ml (8 fl oz) milk
250 ml (8 fl oz) cream
1 large waxy potato, thinly sliced
pinch of freshly grated nutmeg
1 small carrot, thinly sliced
1 small swede, thinly sliced
¹/2 parsnip, thinly sliced
1 small turnip, thinly sliced
105 g (3¹/2 oz) Gruyère cheese, grated

1 Melt the butter in a pan, add the garlic and cook over low heat for 1 minute. Add the milk, cream, potato, nutmeg, a pinch of salt and some black pepper. Bring to the boil and cook, covered, for 5 minutes. Add the carrot and cook for 3 minutes, then add the swede and cook for 3 minutes. Add the parsnip and cook for another 3 minutes, then finally add the turnip and cook for 2 minutes. The vegetables should be tender, but still have a little resistance when tested with the point of a sharp knife. Strain the cooking liquid from the vegetables and reserve.

2 Preheat the oven to moderate 180°C (350°F/Gas 4). Butter a 1.5 litre shallow gratin or ovenproof dish. Layer the vegetables in the prepared dish and pour over some of the reserved cooking liquid to barely cover. Sprinkle with the cheese and bake for 20–25 minutes, or until the vegetables are tender and the surface is golden. Stand for 10 minutes before serving.

Pumpkin purée (left) and Gratin of root vegetables

Traditional Christmas pudding

This richest of fruit puddings needs no introduction. We have given two traditional methods—boiling and steaming—and both are easy to make in advance and can be reheated easily on Christmas day.

Preparation time **45 minutes + overnight marinating**
Total cooking time **10–12 hours**
Serves 8

☗

MARINATED FRUITS
250 g (8 oz) sultanas
250 g (8 oz) raisins
315 g (10 oz) currants
60 g (2 oz) glacé cherries
60 g (2 oz) candied mixed peel
60 g (2 oz) dates, stoned and chopped
1¹/₂ teaspoons mixed spice
1 teaspoon ground cinnamon
1 teaspoon ground nutmeg
¹/₄ teaspoon ground ginger
grated rind of 2 oranges and juice of 1 orange
grated rind of 1 lemon
105 ml (3¹/₂ fl oz) stout
125 ml (4 fl oz) brandy

PUDDING
150 g (5 oz) apples, peeled, cored and grated
150 g (5 oz) plain flour
105 g (3¹/₂ oz) ground almonds
200 g (6¹/₂ oz) suet, shredded
150 g (5 oz) dark brown sugar
200 g (6¹/₂ oz) fresh white breadcrumbs
2 eggs, beaten
2 tablespoons treacle

3 tablespoons brandy

1 To make the marinated fruits, place all the ingredients into a large bowl and mix together well. Cover with plastic wrap and leave overnight in a cool place.
2 The next day, prepare the pudding by placing all the ingredients in a bowl and making a well in the centre. Add the marinated fruits and mix to form a soft batter.
3 To boil the pudding, place a 70 cm (28 inch) square of calico or a tea towel in a pan of water and bring to the boil. Drain, then squeeze out wearing rubber gloves. Wrap the pudding following the method in Chef's techniques on page 61. Bring a pan of water to the boil, large enough for the pudding to move around in and with a saucer or trivet at the bottom. Place the pudding in the pan, cover and boil for 10–12 hours.
4 Remove the pudding from the pan and remove the string. Leave for 5 minutes, then loosen the cloth, turn the pudding out onto a plate and gently peel away the cloth.
5 To steam the pudding, brush one 2.5 litre pudding basin with melted butter and line the base with a disc of baking paper. Lay a sheet of foil on the work surface, cover with a sheet of baking paper, and make a large pleat in the middle. Grease the paper with melted butter.
6 Place the mixture in the basin and hollow the surface with the back of a wet spoon. Place the foil, paper-side-down, across the top and tie string securely around the rim and over the top to make a handle. Place a saucer or trivet in a pan and rest the pudding basin on it. Half-fill the pan with boiling water and bring to the boil. Cover and simmer for 10 hours, topping up the water if needed with more boiling water. Stand for 15 minutes, then remove the string, foil and paper and turn out.
7 In a small pan, warm the brandy, then at the table pour it over the pudding and ignite it at arm's length. Serve with cream or brandy butter (see page 35).

Chef's tip To prepare ahead of time, steam or boil the pudding for 8 hours, then leave to cool (for the boiled pudding, hang up to dry overnight). Remove the cloth or paper and check the surface is completely dry. Re-cover with dry cloth or new paper and store somewhere cool. To reheat, cook for 2 hours, then leave for 15 minutes.

Quick microwave Christmas pudding

You don't have to miss out on the traditional finale to Christmas lunch just because you're short of time. This fruit-filled version is ready to eat in less than an hour and can be prepared well in advance.

*Preparation time **45 minutes***
*Total cooking time **20 minutes + 20 minutes standing***
Serves 8

☼

90 g (3 oz) plain flour
90 g (3 oz) suet, shredded
2 teaspoons mixed spice
¹/₂ teaspoon ground cinnamon
45 g (1¹/₂ oz) fresh white breadcrumbs
120 g (4 oz) soft brown sugar
60 g (2 oz) ground almonds
1 dessert apple, peeled, cored and
chopped
grated rind of 1 lemon
grated rind of 1 orange
60 g (2 oz) chopped mixed
candied peel
60 g (2 oz) glacé cherries
90 g (3 oz) currants
90 g (3 oz) raisins
155 g (5 oz) sultanas
3 tablespoons golden syrup
1 tablespoon treacle
80 ml (2³/4 fl oz) brandy
105 ml (3¹/2 fl oz) milk
2 eggs

1 Brush a 1.5 litre non-metallic microwavable pudding basin, preferably with a lid, with melted butter. Cut a disc of baking paper to fit the base and another the same size as the top. Place the smaller disc in the base.

2 In a bowl, place the flour, suet, spices, breadcrumbs, brown sugar, almonds and a pinch of salt. Mix with a wooden spoon, then stir in the apple and lemon and orange rind. Add the candied peel, glacé cherries, currants, raisins and sultanas and stir again to mix in.

3 Place the syrup and treacle in a non-metallic microwavable bowl and microwave (based on a 700–800 watt microwave) on low for 30 seconds, or until fluid but not hot. Stir in the brandy, then whisk in the milk and eggs with a fork until smooth. Drizzle the syrup mixture over the dry ingredients and mix thoroughly.

4 Transfer the mixture to the pudding basin, top with the large disc of baking paper and cover with the lid or plastic wrap. Microwave on high for 5 minutes, then stand for 5 minutes. Microwave on high for a further 5 minutes, then stand for 5 minutes. Cool, then store until required.

5 To serve, remove the lid from the basin, sprinkle the surface of the pudding with a tablespoon of water, then cover with plastic wrap. Microwave for 4 minutes on high, leave to stand for 5 minutes, then cook for 3 minutes on high. Stand for 3 minutes before turning out onto a plate. Serve with cream or brandy butter (see page 35).

Whisky sauce

This is a great sauce for Christmas puddings and desserts, flavoured with fresh vanilla and whisky.

Preparation time **15 minutes**
Total cooking time **25 minutes**
Makes 600 ml (20 fl oz)

☼

600 ml (20 fl oz) milk
a large pinch of ground nutmeg
1 vanilla pod, split lengthways
30 g (1 oz) unsalted butter
30 g (1 oz) plain flour
2 tablespoons sugar
2 egg yolks
2 tablespoons cream or milk
3 tablespoons whisky

1 Place the milk in a pan with the nutmeg. Scrape the seeds from the vanilla pod and add to the milk with the pod. Heat gently until small bubbles appear around the edge of the pan. Set aside to cool, then strain the milk, discard the pod and wipe out the pan.

2 Melt the butter in the pan over low heat. Sprinkle the flour over the butter and cook, stirring continuously with a wooden spoon, for 1–2 minutes, without allowing it to colour.

3 Remove from the heat and slowly add the vanilla milk, whisking or beating vigorously to avoid lumps. Return to low heat and bring slowly to the boil, stirring constantly. Add the sugar, then simmer for 3–4 minutes.

4 In a bowl, stir together the egg yolks and cream or milk, then pour on a quarter of the hot sauce, stir together to blend and return the mixture to the remaining sauce in the pan. Add the whisky and stir constantly over low heat to heat through, without allowing the sauce to boil. Add more sugar or whisky, to taste, and strain the sauce. Serve warm.

Brandy butter

The classic partner for Christmas pudding, brandy butter also tastes wonderful with fruit mince pies.

Preparation time **20 minutes**
Total cooking time **Nil**
Makes 250 ml (8 fl oz)

☼

120 g (4 oz) unsalted butter, at room temperature
120 g (4 oz) soft brown sugar
2–3 tablespoons brandy

1 Place the butter in a bowl and whisk using electric beaters or beat with a wooden spoon until soft and creamy. Add the brown sugar a tablespoon at a time, whisking well between additions, until the mixture is light and creamy.

2 Whisk in the brandy, half a tablespoon at a time. Do not add the brandy too quickly or the mixture will separate. Place in a serving bowl, cover with plastic wrap and refrigerate until needed. Return to room temperature before serving.

Chef's tips For a variation, add a little grated orange rind, or use caster sugar for a lighter flavour.

If you want to make the brandy butter well in advance, you could try placing the butter in a piping bag with a star-shaped nozzle and piping small rosettes onto baking trays lined with greaseproof paper. Freeze until hard and store in a bag in the freezer until needed.

Ice-cream Christmas pudding

A great alternative to the traditional pudding, especially if you have a lot of children at your Christmas gathering. It can also be made in advance and just removed from the freezer 30 minutes before serving.

*Preparation time **30 minutes + 8 hours freezing + overnight freezing***
*Total cooking time **20 minutes***
*Serves **6***

❉ ❉

350 ml (11 fl oz) milk
1 vanilla pod, split lengthways
1 cinnamon stick
4 egg yolks
95 g (3¼ oz) soft brown sugar
200 ml (6½ fl oz) cream, chilled
2 tablespoons brandy
105 g (3½ oz) cooked Christmas pudding, Christmas cake or fruit cake, cut into 1.5 cm (⅝ inch) pieces
45 g (1½ oz) marrons glacés, chopped
45 g (1½ oz) glacé cherries, chopped
45 g (1½ oz) amaretti biscuits, broken into large chunks
185 g (6 oz) dark couverture chocolate or good-quality dark chocolate
30 ml (1 fl oz) peanut or groundnut oil
50 g (1¾ oz) white chocolate
holly sprigs, to decorate

1 Prepare a large bowl of iced water with a smaller bowl inside. Pour the milk into a deep heavy-based pan over medium heat. Scrape the seeds from the vanilla pod and add to the milk with the pod and cinnamon stick. Slowly bring to the boil, then remove from the heat. Place the egg yolks and sugar in a bowl and cream together using electric beaters or a wooden spoon until pale and thick. Strain in the hot milk, discarding the vanilla pod and cinnamon, and mix well. Pour the mixture into a clean pan and cook over extremely low heat, stirring, for 5 minutes, or until it thickens and coats the back of a spoon. If the mixture is getting too hot,

remove from the heat for a few seconds and whisk. Do not boil or it will curdle. Strain into the prepared bowl and cool completely. Stir in the cream and brandy and freeze in a container for 3 hours, or until just firm.

2 Place the mixture in a bowl and beat for 1–2 minutes, or until thick and creamy. Return to the container and refreeze. Repeat the freezing and beating twice more. On the final beating, fold in the pudding, marrons glacés, glacé cherries and amaretti biscuits. Place in a 1 litre rounded pudding basin lined with plastic wrap bigger than the basin, cover with the overhang of plastic wrap and freeze overnight until hard, stirring after 30 minutes if the fruits and pudding have sunk to the bottom.

3 Remove the ice cream from the basin (if it is hard to get out, dip into a bowl of hot water for 5 seconds). Turn out onto a chilled plate and remove the plastic wrap, then freeze again while preparing the topping.

4 To make the topping, bring a pan half full of water to the boil, then remove from the heat. Have ready a heatproof bowl that will fit over the pan without actually touching the water. Put the dark chocolate in the bowl and place over the pan of steaming water. Stir occasionally until the chocolate has melted. Remove the bowl from the pan, add the oil and stir until cool but still flowing. Remove the ice cream from the freezer and set on a wire rack over a tray. Pour the chocolate over it to completely coat in a thin layer, then return to the freezer for 1–2 hours. Move to a serving plate.

5 Melt the white chocolate in the same way as the dark and spoon over the chilled ice-cream cake so that it dribbles slightly down the sides to resemble thick custard on a Christmas pudding. Refrigerate for a few minutes to set the white chocolate, decorate with a sprig of holly and serve immediately.

Chef's tip If you make this in advance, remove from the freezer to the refrigerator 30 minutes before serving.

Chocolate and chestnut mousse

The combination of dark chocolate and chestnut purée makes for a rich, yet silky-textured mousse. Decorate with cream, marrons glacés and a dusting of cocoa to finish off this impressive dessert.

Preparation time **1 hour 30 minutes + 3 hours or overnight chilling**
Total cooking time **30 minutes**
Serves 10–12

SPONGE
1 egg
90 g (3 oz) sugar
15 g (1/2 oz) plain flour
15 g (1/2 oz) cocoa powder
3 tablespoons rum

MOUSSE
90 g (3 oz) caster sugar
3 egg yolks
120 g (4 oz) dark chocolate, roughly chopped
300 g (10 oz) canned, sweet chestnut purée
3 leaves gelatine or 1 1/2 teaspoons gelatine powder
1 tablespoon rum
375 ml (12 fl oz) cream, for whipping

200 ml (6 1/2 fl oz) whipped cream, to decorate
3 marrons glacés, cut into quarters
cocoa, to dust

1 Butter and flour a 17 x 6 cm (7 x 2 1/2 inch) loose-bottomed cake or spring-form tin. Preheat the oven to moderate 180°C (350°F/Gas 4).
2 To make the sponge, place the egg and a third of the sugar in a bowl and whisk until pale and doubled in volume. Sieve together the flour and cocoa and, using a metal spoon or plastic spatula, fold into the egg mixture. Pour into the prepared tin and bake for 12–14 minutes, or until firm to a light touch. Cool on a wire rack, wash the tin and line with a double thickness of baking paper.
3 Place 3 tablespoons water and the remaining sugar in a pan and stir over low heat until the sugar dissolves. Bring to the boil and cook for 1 minute, without stirring, then remove from heat, stir in the rum and cool. Return the cooled sponge to the tin and spoon over the syrup.
4 To make the mousse, place 30 ml (1 fl oz) water and the sugar in a pan and stir over low heat until the sugar has dissolved. Using a wet pastry brush, brush any sugar crystals from the side of the pan. Boil, without stirring, until 1/4 teaspoon of the syrup dropped into a bowl of iced water forms a ball that holds its shape, but is soft when pressed. Place the egg yolks in a bowl and whisk at high speed with electric beaters. Pour the bubbling syrup onto the yolks between the beaters and the side of the bowl. Whisk for 6 minutes, or until cold.
5 Bring a pan half full of water to the boil, then remove from the heat. Have ready a heatproof bowl that fits over the pan without touching the water. Put the chocolate in the bowl and place over the steaming water. Stir occasionally until the chocolate has melted, then remove the bowl and stir in the chestnut purée. Place the gelatine leaves in a bowl and cover with cold water, or dissolve the powder in 1 1/2 tablespoons water. Place the rum in a pan and warm over low heat. Squeeze the water from the leaves, if using, and place the leaves or powder in the rum and over a very low heat, swirl the pan to dissolve. Cool for 1 minute, then strain onto the chocolate and stir together. Lightly whip the cream until it leaves a firm trail as it falls from the whisk.
6 Using a spatula, fold the cream and the chestnut mixture alternately into the egg yolk mixture until there are no streaks, then pour on top of the sponge. Tap the tin on the work surface to release any air bubbles, then smooth the surface. Chill for 3 hours or overnight.
7 Remove the tin from the mousse and place the whipped cream in a piping bag. Mark into 10–12 portions and pipe three bulbs of cream in each. Place a marron glacé quarter on each outside bulb and dust with cocoa.

Galette des rois

This is the traditional Twelfth Night cake, which contains a lucky bean that represents the baby Jesus. The person who finds the bean becomes king or queen for the day. During the winter holidays, these cakes can be seen adorned with gold crowns in French patisseries.

*Preparation time **2 hours + 1 hour 10 minutes chilling***
*Total cooking time **50 minutes***
*Serves **6–8***

ALMOND CREAM
50 g (1³/4 oz) unsalted butter, at room temperature
50 g (1³/4 oz) icing sugar, sifted
2 teaspoons finely grated lemon rind
1 egg yolk, beaten
50 g (1³/4 oz) ground almonds, sieved
1 tablespoon plain flour
1–2 teaspoons rum

CUSTARD
250 ml (8 fl oz) milk
1/2 vanilla pod
2 egg yolks
55 g (1³/4 oz) caster sugar
1 tablespoon cornflour

2 x 375 g (12 oz) blocks ready-made puff pastry, thawed
2 egg yolks, beaten
45 g (1¹/2 oz) caster sugar

1 To make the almond cream, beat the butter, sugar and lemon rind together using a wooden spoon or electric beaters, until light and creamy. Add the egg yolk, a third at a time, beating well between each addition. Stir in the almonds, flour and rum, cover and refrigerate.

2 To make the custard, prepare a bowl of iced water with a shallow bowl inside. Pour the milk into a pan. Scrape the seeds from the vanilla pod and add to the milk with the pod. Slowly bring to the boil, then remove from the heat. Place the yolks and sugar in a bowl and, using a balloon whisk or electric beaters, cream together, until pale and thick, then whisk in the cornflour. Strain in the hot milk, discarding the pod, and mix well. Pour into a clean pan and slowly bring to the boil, whisking continuously. When boiling, strain into the prepared bowl and cool completely, then whisk until smooth and fold into the almond cream with a spoon. Cover and refrigerate.

3 Roll each block of pastry to a 5 mm (¹/4 inch) thick, 27 cm (11 inch) square. Place each sheet of pastry onto a baking tray lined with baking paper and refrigerate for 5 minutes. Place the custard and almond mixture into a piping bag fitted with a large plain nozzle.

4 Using plates as a guide, cut a 20 cm (8 inch) circle and a 22 cm (9 inch) circle from the pastry. Pipe the mixture in a spiral onto the smaller circle, starting from the middle and finishing about 2.5 cm (1 inch) from the edge. Repeat to form a slightly smaller circle over the one you have just piped. Brush the outer edge of the pastry with water. Place the larger circle over the cream, without trapping any air underneath the pastry, and seal the flat, outer edge with thumb and finger.

5 Brush the top with the beaten egg yolk and chill for 45 minutes. Brush again and chill for 20 minutes. Preheat the oven to moderately hot 200°C (400°F/Gas 6). Score the top with the back of a knife in a spiral spoke pattern, then bake for 30–35 minutes, or until a knife inserted horizontally into the side comes out clean. Remove, then increase the oven to very hot 230°C (450°F/Gas 8).

6 Place the sugar and 45 ml (1¹/2 fl oz) water in a pan and stir to the boil, then boil hard for 5 minutes, or until syrupy but not coloured. Brush the top of the warm galette with the syrup and bake for 5 minutes. Cool completely on a wire rack, then serve in thin wedges.

Chef's tip To make a traditional galette, hide a dried bean or pottery token in the filling and cut out a crown from gold card to place on top.

Yule log

Not only fun for children to help make, this traditional French Christmas cake is perfect for an indulgent tea time, and the adults won't be able to resist either.

Preparation time **2 hours**
Total cooking time **30 minutes**
Serves **8–10**

SPONGE
4 large eggs
120 g (4 oz) caster sugar
90 g (3 oz) plain flour
30 g (1 oz) cocoa powder

PRALINE BUTTER CREAM
25 g (³/4 oz) skinned hazelnuts
25 g (³/4 oz) blanched whole almonds
175 g (5³/4 oz) caster sugar
2 egg yolks
290 g (9¹/2 oz) unsalted butter, beaten to soften

GANACHE
50 ml (1³/4 fl oz) cream
250 g (8 oz) good-quality dark chocolate,
    finely chopped
30 g (1 oz) unsalted butter, beaten to soften

ready-made marzipan, to decorate
red and green food colouring, to decorate

1 Preheat the oven to very hot 230°C (450°F/Gas 8). Line a 25 x 30 cm (10 x 12 inch) swiss roll tin with baking paper. Bring a pan half full of water to the boil, then remove from the heat. Have ready a heatproof bowl that fits over the pan without touching the water.
2 To make the sponge, put the eggs and sugar in the bowl and place over the pan of water. Whisk until thick, pale and three or four times the original volume. Remove the bowl and whisk for 2 minutes until cold. Sieve the flour and cocoa onto the surface and, using a metal spoon, fold in until just incorporated. Spread into the tin and bake for 2–3 minutes, or until the surface is just firm. Transfer on the paper to a wire rack. Reduce the oven temperature to moderate 180°C (350°F/Gas 4).
3 To make the praline butter cream, put the nuts on a baking tray and cook for 8 minutes, or until light golden. Place 45 g (1¹/2 oz) of the sugar in a heavy-based pan and stir over low heat until melted, then raise the heat to medium and cook, without stirring, to a golden caramel. Remove from the heat, quickly stir in the nuts, then tip onto a lightly oiled baking tray. Flatten slightly with the back of a spoon and leave until completely cold.
4 Place 3 tablespoons water and the remaining sugar in a pan and stir over low heat until the sugar has dissolved. Using a wet pastry brush, brush any sugar crystals from the side of the pan. Boil, without stirring, until ¹/4 teaspoon of the syrup dropped into a bowl of iced water forms a ball that holds its shape, but is soft when pressed. Place the yolks in a bowl and whisk at high speed with electric beaters. Pour the bubbling syrup onto the yolks between the beaters and the side of the bowl. Whisk for 6 minutes, or until cold. Add the butter and beat until smooth. Using a rolling pin, crush the praline finely and mix in. Cover with plastic wrap and set aside somewhere cool.
5 To make the ganache, bring the cream to the boil in a pan. Remove from the heat and whisk in the chocolate until melted, then whisk in the butter until smooth.
6 To assemble the log, turn the sponge over, remove the paper and spread this side with the ganache, reserving a little. Using the paper, roll up from one long side into a swiss roll and place on a dish. Diagonally cut off one end of the roll and place the cut side at an angle on the log to represent a branch, securing with ganache. Spread the outside with the butter cream and lightly fork to resemble bark. Colour the marzipan with the food colourings, then cut out holly leaves and roll red berries between your fingers to decorate the log.

Iced Christmas cake

This classic Christmas cake can be started in November or early December and iced nearer to the day.
If you are short of time, you can keep the decorations much simpler with just holly leaves and berries.

*Preparation time **3 hours + 1 week and***
*   **2 overnight standings***
*Total cooking time **3 hours***
Serves 10

❄ ❄

95 g (3¹/4 oz) currants
250 g (8 oz) sultanas
95 g (3¹/4 oz) raisins
60 g (2 oz) chopped mixed peel
60 g (2 oz) glacé cherries
160 g (5¹/4 oz) plain flour
120 g (4 oz) unsalted butter, at room temperature
95 g (3¹/4 oz) soft brown sugar
3 eggs, beaten
grated rind and juice of 1 lemon and 1 orange
¹/2 teaspoon vanilla extract or essence
1 tablespoon black treacle
1 teaspoon ground mixed spice
200 ml (6¹/2 fl oz) rum or brandy
100 g (3¹/4 oz) apricot jam
500 g (1 lb) ready-made marzipan
clear alcohol, such as gin or vodka, for brushing
1.5 kg (3 lb) ready-made soft icing
1 egg white, for royal icing
200 g (6¹/2 oz) icing sugar, sifted, for royal icing
juice of ¹/2 lemon, for royal icing
red, green and yellow food colouring

1 Double line a 20 cm (8 inch) round cake tin following the method in the Chef's techniques on page 62. Preheat the oven to warm 160°C (315°F/Gas 2–3).

2 Place the fruit in a bowl and mix in half the flour. Beat the butter and sugar until light and creamy. Add the egg in additions, beating well between each addition. Beat in the lemon and orange rind and juice, the vanilla and treacle. Sift the remaining flour and mixed spice onto the butter mixture and beat well. Stir in the fruit.

3 Place the mixture in the prepared tin and make a dip in the centre with the back of a wet spoon. Bake for about 3 hours, or until a skewer inserted into the centre comes out clean. Cover with foil if it is browning too quickly. Cool in the tin on a wire rack, then make several holes in the cake with a skewer.

4 Without removing the paper, wrap the cake tightly in plastic wrap and store in a cool place for at least 1 week, soaking with a little of the rum or brandy regularly.

5 Level the surface of the cake with a sharp knife, then turn base-up. In a small pan, melt the jam and brush over the cake, then place on a thin 20 cm (8 inch) board. Marzipan and ice the cake following the method in the Chef's techniques on page 63.

6 To decorate the cake, pull a walnut-size piece of icing from the remaining soft icing and colour it yellow. Make a small star and present shape. Divide the remaining icing into two thirds and one third. Colour the larger amount green and the smaller red. Cover and set aside the red. Roll out the green icing to a 2 mm (¹/8 inch) thickness on a surface dusted with icing sugar. Cut out a 1 x 75 cm (¹/2 x 30 inch) ribbon, cover and set aside. Cut out 8 holly leaves. Gather together the remaining icing, colour a darker green and form a Christmas tree by making a cone shape and randomly snipping the sides with scissors. Take the red icing and make a red ribbon, 12 holly berries and a small present to go under the tree.

7 Twist the two pieces of ribbon together and wrap around the cake, fixing with some of the reserved royal icing at four intervals to give a drape effect. At each fixed point, stick on two holly leaves and three berries. Leave to dry overnight.

8 The next day, arrange the tree and presents on top of the cake. Mix the remaining royal icing with the food colourings and pipe 'Merry Christmas' onto the centre of the cake and extra decorations on the tree and presents.

Fruit mince pies

Home-made fruit mince pies are the traditional accompaniment to drinks when guests come round over Christmas. These ones are made with meltingly short pastry and a brandy-laced mincemeat.

Preparation time **1 hour + 40 minutes chilling**
   (make the mincemeat 1 week in advance)
Total cooking time **20 minutes**
Makes 12

MINCEMEAT (see Chef's tip)
250 g (8 oz) suet, shredded
250 g (8 oz) cooking apples, peeled, cored
   and roughly chopped
120 g (4 oz) chopped mixed peel
250 g (8 oz) raisins
250 g (8 oz) sultanas
250 g (8 oz) currants
25 g (3/4 oz) slivered almonds
185 g (6 oz) demerara sugar
1/2 teaspoon ground mixed spice
large pinch ground nutmeg
large pinch ground cinnamon
finely grated rind and juice of 1/2 lemon
80 ml (23/4 fl oz) brandy

SHORTCRUST PASTRY
185 g (6 oz) plain flour
115 g (33/4 oz) unsalted butter, chilled
   and cut into cubes
25 g (3/4 oz) hard white fat, such as lard, chilled
   and cut into cubes
1 egg yolk
2 drops vanilla extract or essence

caster sugar, to dust

1 To make the mincemeat, place the suet, apple, mixed peel and raisins in a food processor and, using the pulse button, break down roughly. Place in a large bowl, add the remaining ingredients and stir to combine well.

2 Spoon the mincemeat into four x 500 ml (16 fl oz) sterilized preserving jars or jars with screw-top lids, pressing down to force out any air. Screw the lids on tightly and store in the refrigerator for at least 1 week.

3 To make the pastry, sift the flour and some salt into a large bowl and add the butter and lard. Using a fast, light, flicking action of thumb across fingertips, rub the butter and lard into the flour until the mixture resembles fine breadcrumbs. Make a well in the centre. In a bowl, mix together the egg yolk, vanilla and 1 1/2 tablespoons water and pour into the well. Mix with a round-bladed knife until large lumps form. Pull together and turn out onto a lightly floured surface. Knead very gently for no more than 20 seconds until just smooth, then wrap in plastic wrap and refrigerate for at least 20 minutes.

4 Brush a 12-hole shallow patty pan or tart tray with melted butter. Preheat the oven to moderately hot 200°C (400°F/Gas 6). On a lightly floured surface, roll out two thirds of the pastry to a 3 mm (1/8 inch) thickness. Using an 8 cm (3 inch) cutter, cut out circles and ease into the holes by pressing lightly. Chill while rolling out the remaining pastry as above. Using a 7 cm (23/4 inch) cutter, cut circles for the top of each pie. Place on a plastic-wrap-lined tray and chill for 20 minutes.

5 Fill each pastry-lined hole with 1 tablespoon of mincemeat. Take the pastry circles, brush the outer edges with water, then place, damp-side-down, on the mincemeat. Gently press the top and bottom pastry edges together to seal. Brush the tops with cold water and lightly dust with the sugar. Using the point of a sharp knife, make a small hole in the centre of each.

6 Bake for 20 minutes, or until golden. Serve hot with cream or brandy butter (see page 35).

Chef's tip The mincemeat is best left to mature over a few weeks or months. Any unopened jars should be stored in cool, dark and dry conditions or the refrigerator.

Stollen

This sweet, yeasty German Christmas bread is usually baked several weeks before Christmas to allow the flavour of the spices to mature. When cooked, it is liberally brushed with butter for a delicious crust.

Preparation time 1 hour + 4 hours proving + overnight marinating
Total cooking time 45 minutes
Makes 2 stollen (each cuts into 16 slices)

1 teaspoon ground mixed spice
155 g (5 oz) chopped mixed peel
45 g (1¹/2 oz) glacé cherries, quartered
60 g (2 oz) flaked almonds
2 tablespoons rum
grated rind of 2 small lemons
155 g (5 oz) raisins
90 ml (3 fl oz) milk
30 g (1 oz) fresh yeast or 15 g (¹/2 oz) dried yeast
375 g (12 oz) plain flour
55 g (1³/4 oz) caster sugar
185 g (6 oz) unsalted butter
1 egg, beaten
250 g (8 oz) ready-made marzipan
1 egg and 1 egg yolk, beaten, for brushing
30 g (1 oz) unsalted butter, melted
icing sugar, to dust

1 Mix the spice, peel, cherries, almonds, rum, lemon rind and raisins together. Cover and marinate overnight.
2 Put the milk in a small pan and heat until tepid. Pour into a bowl and dissolve the yeast in it. Sift 125 g (4 oz) of the plain flour and 1¹/2 teaspoons of the sugar into a bowl. Make a well in the centre and pour in the yeast mixture. Mix to a smooth paste, then cover with plastic wrap. Leave in a warm place for 40 minutes, or until doubled in size.
3 Using your fingertips, rub the butter into the remaining flour until the mixture resembles fine breadcrumbs, then stir in the remaining sugar and

¹/2 teaspoon salt. Pour in the beaten egg and mix well.
4 Add the proved yeast mixture to the dough and mix until smooth. Add the marinated ingredients and stir in, then turn the mixture out onto a lightly floured work surface and knead to a smooth elastic dough. Place the dough in a large lightly floured bowl, cover with a damp cloth and prove in a warm place for 2–2¹/2 hours, or until doubled in size.
5 Brush two large baking trays with melted butter and set aside. Cut the marzipan in half and roll out both halves on a surface lightly dusted with icing sugar to form two 20 x 2.5 cm (8 x 1 inch) cylinders.
6 Turn the dough out onto a lightly floured surface and knead gently for 2 minutes, or until smooth once more, then divide in half. Roll each piece into a rectangle about 22 x 25 cm (9 x 10 inches), and place a cylinder of marzipan down the centre of each. Sprinkle with a few drops of water and close the dough around the marzipan, sealing the edges by pressing them together. Place on the prepared baking trays, seam-side-down, cover with a damp cloth and prove for 50 minutes, or until doubled in size. Preheat the oven to moderate 180°C (350°F/Gas 4). Lightly brush the stollen with the beaten egg and bake for 35–45 minutes, or until well risen and golden.
7 Remove from the oven and, while the stollen is still warm, brush with the melted butter and dust liberally with icing sugar. Transfer to a wire rack to cool completely, then slice to serve.

Chef's tips This recipe makes two stollen, which is perfect if you are baking for a large Christmas gathering. Otherwise, wrap one in plastic wrap, then foil, and freeze for up to 3 months.

A stollen makes a lovely Christmas gift, wrapped in cellophane and tied with ribbon.

Sherry trifle

This famous British dessert is a Christmas tradition, with its sherry-soaked sponge, red fruit and rich custard. If you prefer a non-alcoholic version, substitute orange juice for the sherry.

Preparation time **55 minutes +**
1 hour 20 minutes chilling
Total cooking time **30 minutes**
Serves 8

SPONGE

3 eggs
90 g (3 oz) caster sugar
55 g (1³/4 oz) plain flour
150 g (5 oz) raspberry jam

2–3 tablespoons sweet sherry
150 g (5 oz) fresh or frozen raspberries
150 g (5 oz) fresh or frozen blackberries
500 ml (16 fl oz) cream
25 g (³/4 oz) icing sugar
¹/4 teaspoon vanilla extract or essence
2 tablespoons pistachio nuts, chopped
8 strawberries, halved

CUSTARD

500 ml (16 fl oz) milk
35 g (1¹/4 oz) custard powder
75 g (2¹/2 oz) caster sugar
165 ml (5¹/2 fl oz) cream

1 Preheat the oven to hot 220°C (425°F/Gas 7). Brush a 25 x 30 cm (10 x 12 inch) swiss roll tin with melted butter, line the base with baking paper and brush again with melted butter.
2 To make the sponge, bring a pan half full of water to the boil, then remove from the heat. Have ready a heatproof bowl that will fit over the pan without actually touching the water. Place the eggs and sugar in the bowl, then place over the pan of simmering water.

Beat for 4 minutes, or until pale, trebled in volume and when lifted on the beaters, the mixture falls back to leave a ribbon-like trail. Remove the bowl from the pan and continue beating for 2 minutes, or until the mixture is cold. Sieve the flour onto the mixture and, using a large metal spoon, fold in until just combined. Pour into the prepared tin, lightly level with a palette knife and bake for 6 minutes, or until pale golden and springy to the touch of a finger. Slide in its paper onto a rack and leave to cool, then turn over onto a clean piece of greaseproof paper and remove the paper on which it was baked. Spread the sponge thinly with jam and, using the paper, roll up from one long side into a swiss roll. Wrap in greaseproof paper and chill for 20 minutes.
3 Discard the paper and, using a serrated or sharp knife, cut into 5 mm (¹/4 inch) slices. Arrange the slices across the base and up the side of a large glass bowl with a wide, flat base. Fill the centre with any remaining slices, then drizzle the sherry over the sponge and add the raspberries and blackberries, levelling the top. Cover the bowl with plastic wrap and chill until required.
4 To make the custard, bring the milk almost to the boil in a deep, heavy-based pan. Place the custard powder and sugar in a bowl, add the cream and quickly whisk to blend and prevent lumps. Whisk in about one third of hot milk, then pour the mixture back into the pan. Bring to the boil over low-medium heat, whisking vigorously, then remove from the heat. Continue to gently whisk for about 5 minutes while the custard cools to a warm but still flowing mixture, then pour onto the fruit. Cover the surface with plastic wrap and chill for at least 1 hour.
5 Whisk together the cream, icing sugar and vanilla until soft peaks form. Decorate the trifle with this cream mixture and top with the nuts and strawberries. Chill until ready to serve.

Panforte

A speciality of Sienna in Italy, this spiced sweetmeat should be served with strong coffee.

Preparation time **20 minutes**
Total cooking time **35 minutes**
Serves 12

❖

2 sheets rice paper
45 g (1 1/2 oz) dark chocolate, roughly chopped
1 small cinnamon stick
4 cloves
4 black peppercorns
3/4 teaspoon grated nutmeg
180 g (5 3/4 oz) soft brown sugar
90 g (3 oz) clear honey
280 g (9 oz) unskinned whole almonds, roasted
25 g (3/4 oz) walnuts, roasted
25 g (3/4 oz) hazelnuts, skinned and roasted
115 g (3 3/4 oz) plain flour, sifted
375 g (12 oz) mixed candied fruit, chopped
icing sugar, to dust

1 Preheat the oven to moderate 180°C (350°F/Gas 4). Grease a 20 x 2.5 cm (8 x 1 inch) cake tin with a removable base. Line the base and side with rice paper.
2 Bring a pan half full of water to the boil, then remove from the heat. Put the chocolate in a bowl inside the pan, ensuring it is not touching the water. Stir occasionally until the chocolate melts, then remove the bowl. Grind the cinnamon, cloves and peppercorns until powdered and stir into the chocolate with the nutmeg.
3 Place the sugar and honey in a pan and stir slowly to the boil, then boil for 30 seconds, stirring. Remove from the heat and mix in the nuts, flour, candied fruit and chocolate. Press the mixture into the cake tin, flatten with the back of a wet spoon and bake for 30 minutes.
4 Cool in the tin for 5 minutes, then remove the tin, leaving the rice paper on the panforte. Cool on a wire rack, then turn over and dust with icing sugar.

Biscotti

These nutty, spicy little biscuits are traditionally served to be dipped into a glass of sweet wine.

Preparation time **25 minutes**
Total cooking time **1 hour 50 minutes**
Makes about 30 biscuits

❖

3 eggs
275 g (9 oz) caster sugar
1 teaspoon vanilla extract or essence
finely grated rind of 2 lemons
425 g (13 1/2 oz) plain flour
2 teaspoons baking powder
1/2 teaspoon ground mixed spice
155 g (5 oz) unskinned whole almonds, roughly chopped
icing sugar, to dust

1 Preheat the oven to warm 160°C (315°F/Gas 2–3). Grease a baking tray and line with baking paper.
2 Bring a pan half full of water to the boil, then remove from the heat. Put the eggs, sugar, vanilla, lemon rind and 1 teaspoon salt in a bowl inside the pan, ensuring it is not touching the water. Whisk until thick and mousse-like and a trail is left when the mixture is lifted on the whisk. Remove the bowl and whisk until the bowl feels cold and the mixture is cold and fluffy.
3 Sift together the flour, baking powder and spice and, using a metal spoon, fold into the egg mixture. When almost blended in, mix in the almonds, turn the dough out onto a lightly floured surface and very lightly knead and form into a long, flattish slipper shape. Transfer to the baking tray and bake for 50 minutes, or until golden. Slide on the paper onto a wire rack to cool.
4 Reduce the oven temperature to very slow 140°C (275°F/Gas 1). Remove the paper from the biscotti and, using a sharp knife, cut into diagonal slices 1 cm (1/2 inch) thick. Place on the baking tray and bake for 55 minutes, or until golden and very dry to the touch. Dust the cooled biscuits with icing sugar, if desired.

Panforte (left) and Biscotti

Dickensian Christmas cobbler

This beautiful fruit pudding is full of spices, fresh and dried fruit and has an old-fashioned, Victorian Christmas feel to it. For a special occasion, set alight with warm brandy at the table.

Preparation time **25 minutes + 20 minutes chilling**
Total cooking time **40 minutes**
Serves 6

FRUIT COMPOTE

1 cinnamon stick
2 cloves
1/2 vanilla pod
3 star anise
4 cardamom pods
75 g (2 1/2 oz) caster or soft light brown sugar
60 g (2 oz) unsalted butter
60 g (2 oz) pitted prunes, halved
60 g (2 oz) dates, stoned and roughly chopped
90 g (3 oz) dried figs, quartered
3 ripe pears, peeled, cored and cut into eighths
3 red plums, stoned and quartered,
    or 3 canned plums, drained
75 g (2 1/2 oz) frozen or fresh cranberries
410 ml (13 fl oz) red wine

TOPPING

310 g (10 oz) plain flour
2 teaspoons baking powder
1/2 teaspoon ground mace
1/2 teaspoon ground cinnamon
1/2 teaspoon ground cloves
1/2 teaspoon ground nutmeg
75 g (2 1/2 oz) unsalted butter, chilled and cut into cubes
45 g (1 1/2 oz) caster sugar
2 eggs, beaten
2 tablespoons milk

1 egg and 1 egg yolk, to glaze
icing sugar, for dusting
3 tablespoons brandy

1 Lightly butter a round 18 x 6 cm (7 x 2 1/2 inch) ovenproof dish.

2 To make the fruit compote, place the cinnamon stick, cloves, vanilla pod, star anise and cardamom pods in a piece of muslin and tie into a bag with some string.

3 In a pan, melt the sugar, then cook until it turns to a golden caramel. Remove from the heat, add the butter, then return to the heat and cook for 2 minutes. Add the prunes, dates, figs, pear and spice bag and cook for about 3–4 minutes, or until the pear is tender. Add the plums, cranberries and wine and stir once to combine, without breaking up the fruit, then bring to a simmer and cook for 2–3 minutes, or until the fruit is just soft. Remove and discard the spice bag. Using a slotted spoon, lift the fruits into the prepared dish. Reheat the liquid and cook to reduce by half, or until a syrupy coating consistency is reached, then pour over. Cool to room temperature.

4 To make the topping, sift the flour, baking powder and spices into a bowl, add the butter and rub in using your fingertips until the mixture resembles fine breadcrumbs. Add the sugar, eggs and milk and, using a palette knife, bring together to form a soft dough. Wrap in plastic wrap and refrigerate for 20 minutes.

5 Preheat the oven to moderate 180°C (350°F/Gas 4). In a small bowl, beat together the egg, egg yolk and a pinch of salt and sugar and set aside.

6 On a lightly floured surface, roll out the dough to a 2 cm (3/4 inch) thickness. Cut out stars with a star-shaped cutter, dipping the cutter into flour occasionally to prevent the dough sticking.

7 Arrange the stars, slightly overlapping, on the fruit around the edge of the dish. Brush the top of the stars with the beaten egg and bake for 15 minutes, or until golden and well risen.

8 Serve hot, dusted with icing sugar. Just before serving, warm the brandy in a pan and ignite at arm's length at the table, pouring on the fruit in the centre of the cobbler.

Stained glass biscuits

Jewel-bright and fun to make, these almond biscuits can be used as decorations for your Christmas tree or prettily wrapped and given out to younger family and guests.

Preparation time **40 minutes + 40 minutes chilling**
Total cooking time **25 minutes**
Makes 10–12

45 g (1¹/₂ oz) unsalted butter
1 teaspoon finely grated lemon rind
45 g (1¹/₂ oz) caster sugar
¹/₂ beaten egg
45 g (1¹/₂ oz) ground almonds
110 g (3³/₄ oz) plain flour
250 g (8 oz) caster sugar, extra
red, green and yellow food colouring

1 Preheat the oven to moderate 180°C (350°F/Gas 4). Brush two baking trays with melted butter and dust lightly with flour.

2 Using a wooden spoon or electric beaters, cream together the butter, lemon rind and sugar until light and fluffy. Add the egg, a little at a time, beating well after each addition. Sift together the almonds and flour, add to the mixture and stir together to form a rough dough. Gather into a ball, wrap in plastic wrap, flatten slightly and refrigerate for 30 minutes. Roll out the dough between two sheets of greaseproof paper to about a 3 mm (¹/₈ inch) thickness.

3 Using a 6 cm (2¹/₂ inch) round cutter, cut out about 10–12 biscuits and transfer as many as fit comfortably onto the prepared trays. Using a 1 cm (¹/₂ inch) round cutter or the narrower end of a 1 cm (¹/₂ inch) piping nozzle, cut out three holes from each biscuit. Chill for 10 minutes.

4 Bake the biscuits for 10 minutes, or until golden brown. Cool on the trays, then place on two lightly oiled baking trays.

5 Place the extra sugar in a small pan with 125 ml (4 fl oz) water and stir over low heat until the sugar dissolves and forms a syrup. Raise the heat to medium and boil the syrup for 10 minutes, or until it just begins to turn golden around the edges of the pan. Pour into three heatproof bowls or small pans and colour each one separately with a few drops of food colouring, stirring once to evenly mix. Using a dessertspoon, carefully spoon a little of the hot syrups into each biscuit hole to give a stained-glass-window effect. If the syrups cool and begin to set, gently rewarm over low heat. If they start to crystallize, add 1–2 tablespoons of liquid glucose or a squeeze of lemon juice.

Chef's tips These biscuits look great hanging from the Christmas tree—make an extra hole before baking to thread with ribbon.

Store the biscuits in a dry place to prevent the stained glass sugar becoming sticky.

Mulled wine

The recipe below is just a guideline—adjust the quantities of wine and sugar to make it as strong or sweet as you like.

*Preparation time **25 minutes + 30 minutes standing**
Total cooking time **5 minutes**
Serves 6–8*

☀

2 oranges
1/2 lemon
1 litre good-quality red wine
2 cinnamon sticks
6 cloves
3–4 blades of mace or a pinch of ground mace
6 tablespoons caster sugar

1 Using a potato peeler or sharp knife, thinly pare the rind from the oranges and lemon without taking off any white pith. Squeeze the juice from the oranges.
2 Place the remaining ingredients with the rind and orange juice into a large stainless steel or non-reactive pan and, over medium heat, bring to simmering point. Remove from the heat and allow the wine to stand and infuse for 30 minutes.
3 When ready to serve, reheat the mulled wine gently, then strain into a jug, discard the flavourings and serve warm in glasses.

Egg nog

Also known as an egg flip, this nourishing alcoholic drink is a Christmas tradition, especially on the morning after an indulgent evening.

*Preparation time **45 minutes + 20 minutes chilling**
Total cooking time **Nil**
Serves 12*

☀

100 g (3 1/4 oz) sugar
6 eggs, separated
100 ml (3 1/4 fl oz) bourbon
100 ml (3 1/4 fl oz) brandy
300 ml (10 fl oz) full-fat milk
3/4 teaspoon ground nutmeg
100 ml (3 1/4 fl oz) cream, for whipping
1/4 teaspoon ground nutmeg, to finish

1 In a large bowl, whisk the sugar and egg yolks until thick and very pale in colour.
2 Add the bourbon and brandy in small amounts, beating between additions (if added too quickly, the alcohol will thin the yolk mixture and it will separate). Cover with plastic wrap and chill for 20 minutes.
3 Just before serving, stir in the milk and nutmeg. In a clean, dry bowl, whisk the egg whites until they just form soft peaks. In a separate bowl, whisk the cream until it just holds peaks. With a large metal spoon or plastic spatula, fold the cream into the mixture, followed by the egg white.
4 Serve immediately in wine glasses and sprinkle with a little nutmeg. If left to stand, stir before serving.

Mulled wine (left) and Egg nog

Chef's techniques

Preparing a poached salmon

Removing the blood line from the cavity gets rid of any bitterness.

Lift up the gill flap behind the cheek of the head and, using kitchen scissors, remove the dark, frilly gills. Repeat on the other side of the fish.

If any scales remain, hold the tail and, using the back of a knife, scrape the skin at a slight angle, working towards the head. Trim the fins. Cut across the tail to shorten it by half, then cut a V shape into the tail.

Wash the salmon under cold water and open it on the belly side where the fishmonger has slit it. Remove the blood line lying along the backbone using a spoon. Rinse and wipe inside and out with paper towels.

To poach without a fish kettle, line a baking dish with a treble layer of foil, 10 cm (4 inches) larger than the salmon. Add the fish and pour over the poaching liquid. Cover with the foil and fold and seal the edges tightly.

Serving a salmon

Boning and skinning a salmon makes it easy to serve while keeping it looking good.

Using a sharp knife, cut the skin just above the tail, then through the skin along the back and in front of the gills. Using the knife to help you, work from head to tail to peel off and discard the skin.

Place a serving plate under one side of the greaseproof paper and flip the salmon over onto the plate, using the paper to help you. Remove the rest of the skin. Remove the head if preferred.

Scrape away any dark flesh with a knife. Split down the centre of the top fillet, carefully remove and lay the two quarter fillets each side of the salmon.

Lift out the backbone by peeling it back from the head end. Snip it with scissors just before the tail. Remove any other stray bones and lift up and replace the two fillets.

Carving a turkey

Carving the turkey carefully will allow everyone a good choice of white and dark meat.

Place the turkey breast-side-up on a board. Cut off the wings, then the legs, cutting through the thigh bones that connect the legs to the body.

Hold the turkey steady with a carving fork and slice down diagonally through the breast meat, holding the knife parallel to the rib cage. Repeat on the other side.

Cut through each thigh and drumstick joint. Hold the thigh steady with a fork and carve the thigh meat, keeping the knife parallel to the bone.

Preparing a ham

Skinning and glazing a ham gives it a beautifully caramelized surface.

With a sharp knife, cut a circle in the skin at the top of the ham near the knuckle. Push your thumbs or fingers under the skin and gently pull it from the cut circle and remove.

With a sharp knife, trim the fat to leave a 1 cm (1/2 inch) thickness of fat. Score the fat with cuts crossways and then diagonally to form a diamond pattern. Be careful not to cut the flesh.

To carve the ham, cut a small wedge from the top of the ham and remove. Hold the leg steady with a carving fork and slice evenly towards the knuckle. The slices will increase in size as you carve.

Wrapping a traditional Christmas pudding

Make sure that your cloth is well coated in flour and the string tied tightly so no water can get in.

Lay the boiled cloth out flat and dust generously with flour. Using your hand, smooth the flour evenly onto the cloth. Place the pudding mixture into the centre of the cloth.

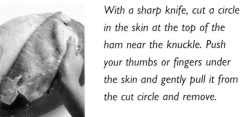

Gather the cloth tightly around the mixture and twist it as tightly as you can to force the mixture into a round ball shape. Tie string around the twisted cloth, as tightly and as close to the pudding as possible.

Boning a quail

*Removing the bones and stuffing the quails
makes them easier to eat.*

Pull off any feathers. Pull the skin back from the neck cavity and cut around the wishbone. Scrape away any meat and cut away at the base. Pull out the wishbone.

Place the quail breast-side-down and cut through the skin down the centre of the back. Using a knife, scrape the flesh away from the carcass, holding the skin as you do so.

When you reach the thigh joints, break the joints so the legs stay attached to the skin and flesh. Continue scraping around the carcass all the way round.

Scrape carefully around the breast bone, and the skin and flesh should come away in one piece. Reserve the carcass.

Double lining a tin

*To protect the crust of fruitcakes with long cooking
times from overcooking, use double lining.*

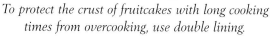
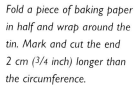

Fold a piece of baking paper in half and wrap around the tin. Mark and cut the end 2 cm (³/4 inch) longer than the circumference.

Cut two circles of baking paper to fit the base of the tin and place one on the bottom of the tin. Snip cuts along the folded edge of the baking paper.

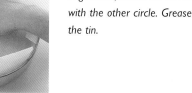

Secure the snipped paper, cut-edge-down, inside the tin. Cover with the other circle. Grease the tin.

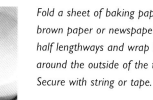

Fold a sheet of baking paper, brown paper or newspaper in half lengthways and wrap it around the outside of the tin. Secure with string or tape.

Marzipan and icing a cake

By using ready-made marzipan and soft icing, decorating the Christmas cake is made easy.

Use small pieces of marzipan to fill in any holes in the cake.

On a surface dusted with icing sugar, roll the remaining marzipan out into a circle large enough to cover the cake. Using a rolling pin, lift it onto the cake.

Ease the marzipan onto the cake, smoothing out any creases. Trim any excess marzipan from around the edge of the cake, then leave to harden overnight.

Brush the marzipan with gin or vodka, then cover with a 4 mm (1/4 inch) layer of soft icing, using the same method as for the marzipan. Trim any excess icing from around the base of the cake.

Brush a 25 cm (10 inch) cake board with alcohol. Roll out the remaining icing and cover the board with a 4 mm (1/4 inch) layer, then trim any excess icing from around the edge. Reserve the remaining icing.

Using two large flat implements, transfer the cake to the centre of the board.

To make the royal icing, beat together the egg white and half the icing sugar to form a smooth paste. Continue adding sugar until thick, then add the lemon juice to soften to a fairly stiff piping consistency.

Set aside a third of the icing, covering the surface with plastic wrap. Place the remaining icing in a piping bag with a small plain nozzle and pipe a decorative edge around the join between the cake and board.

Published by Murdoch Books® a division of Murdoch Magazines Pty Limited, 45 Jones Street, Ultimo NSW 2007.

Murdoch Books and Le Cordon Bleu thank the 32 masterchefs of all the Le Cordon Bleu Schools, whose knowledge and expertise have made this book possible, especially: Chef Terrien, Chef Boucheret, Chef Duchêne (MOF), Chef Guillut, Chef Pinaud, Paris; Chef Males, Chef Walsh, Chef Power, Chef Neveu, Chef Paton, Chef Poole-Gleed, Chef Wavrin, London; Chef Chantefort, Chef Nicaud, Chef Jambert, Chef Honda, Tokyo; Chef Salambien, Chef Boutin, Chef Harris, Sydney; Chef Lawes, Adelaide; Chef Guiet, Chef Denis, Chef Petibon, Chef Jean Michel Poncet, Ottawa.
Of the many students who helped the Chefs test each recipe, a special mention to graduates Hollace Hamilton and Alice Buckley. A very special acknowledgment to Helen Barnard, Alison Oakervee and Deepika Sukhwani, who have been responsible for the coordination of the Le Cordon Bleu team throughout this series under the Presidency of André Cointreau.

Murdoch Books®
Series Manager: Kay Halsey
Series Concept, Design and Art Direction: Juliet Cohen
Food Editor: Lulu Grimes
Designer: Norman Baptista
Photographer: Chris Jones
Food Stylist: Mary Harris
Food Preparation: Kerrie Mullins
Chef's Techniques Photographer: Reg Morrison
Home Economists: Michelle Earl, Michelle Lawton, Kerrie Mullins, Kate Murdoch, Justine Poole, Margot Smithyman

CEO & Publisher: Anne Wilson
Publishing Director: Catie Ziller
General Manager: Mark Smith
Creative Director: Marylouise Brammer
International Sales Director: Mark Newman

National Library of Australia Cataloguing-in-Publication Data
Christmas. ISBN 0 86411 874 0. 1. Christmas cookery. I. Title: Le Cordon Bleu home collection: Christmas.
(Series: Cordon Bleu home collection (Sydney, N.S.W.)). 641.568

Printed by Toppan Printing Hong Kong Co. Ltd. PRINTED IN CHINA
First Printed 1999
©Design and photography Murdoch Books® 1999
©Text Le Cordon Bleu 1999
Distributed in the UK by D Services, 6 Euston Street, Freemen's Common, Leicester LE2 7SS Tel 0116-254-7671 Fax 0116-254-4670. Distributed in Canada by Whitecap (Vancouver) Ltd, 351 Lynn Avenue, North Vancouver, BC V7J 2C4 Tel 604-980-9852 Fax 604-980-8197 or Whitecap (Ontario) Ltd, 47 Coldwater Road, North York, ON M3B 1Y8 Tel 416-444-3442 Fax 416-444-6630

The Publisher and Le Cordon Bleu wish to thank The Bay Tree Kitchen Shop, Pavillion Christofle and Waterford Wedgwood Australia Limited for their assistance with photography
Front cover: Dickensian Christmas cobbler

IMPORTANT INFORMATION

CONVERSION GUIDE

1 cup = 250 ml (8 fl oz)
1 Australian tablespoon = 20 ml (4 teaspoons)
1 UK tablespoon = 15 ml (3 teaspoons)

NOTE: We have used 20 ml tablespoons. If you are using a 15 ml tablespoon, for most recipes the difference will be negligible. For recipes using baking powder, gelatine, bicarbonate of soda and flour, add an extra teaspoon for each tablespoon specified.

CUP CONVERSIONS—DRY INGREDIENTS

1 cup flour, plain or self-raising = 125 g (4 oz)
1 cup sugar, caster = 250 g (8 oz)
1 cup breadcrumbs, dry = 125 g (4 oz)

IMPORTANT: Those who might be at risk from the effects of salmonella food poisoning (the elderly, pregnant women, young children and those suffering from immune deficiency diseases) should consult their GP with any concerns about eating raw eggs.